PENINSULA

Anthology 2022

PENINSULA

First published by Egg Box Publishing in association
with Durham University Part of UEA Publishing Project Ltd
International ©2022 retained by individual authors
A CIO record of this book is available from the British Library
This book is sold subject to the condition that it shall not,
by way of trade or otherwise, be lent, resold, hired out,
stored in retrieval system, or otherwise circulated without
the publisher's prior consent in any form of binding or cover
other than that in which it is published and without a similar
condition including the condition being imposed on the
subsequent purchaser.
Peninsula is typeset in Baskerville Regular
Design and typesetting by Mackenzie Malcolm
Printed and bound in the UK by Imprint Digital
Distributed by NBN International
ISBN 978-1-913861-82-7

INDEX

PENINSULA TEAM	5
EDITORS' NOTE	7
PROSE	
Yusuf Cimcoz	*12*
Jessica Cooper	*20*
Saahiti Shrikant	*30*
Eleni Socratous	*36*
William Woodgate	*46*
POETRY	
Catriona Inglis	*58*
Kate Marshall	*66*
Joanna Morton	*74*
Will Triggs	*84*
AUTHOR BIOS	97

PENINSULA

THE PENINSULA TEAM

EDITORS-IN-CHIEF: Saahiti Shrikant, Eleni Socratous, and Will Triggs

PROSE EDITORS: Yusuf Cimcoz, Jessica Cooper, Saahiti Shrikant, Eleni Socratous

POETRY EDITORS: Catriona Inglis, Will Triggs

ART & DESIGN: Joanna Morton, Yusuf Cimcoz

PUBLICITY COORDINATOR: Catriona Inglis

PROOFREADING: Jessica Cooper, Kate Marshall, William Woodgate

PENINSULA

EDITORS' NOTE

On the east bank of the River Wear, nestled beneath Durham Cathedral, there is a chair — a storyteller's chair. The kind of chair from which countless stories have emerged: stories of knights and dragons, of mystery and intrigue, of metamorphosis and rebirth. In a senseless world, literature is the thread that has always held us together.

Our Peninsula predecessors told stories of 'the great indoors', responding to the experience of living through a global pandemic. A year later, crossing the threshold into a recovering world, we have embraced the opportunity to write with no restrictions, embarking on new journeys of creative liberation. It is in this spirit that we chose our cover-art: a rendition of Palma Studio's In Our Hearts Blind Hope, an installation for Durham's 2021 Lumiere Festival. To us, this stunning projection presented a vision of the beauty that can emerge from the ashes of isolation — and we are very grateful to Joanna Morton for capturing this beauty in acrylics.

From the ashes of zoom call lectures and socially-distanced seminars, this year of transition from virtual to real has brought us not only genuine connection, but lasting friendships. With our Creative Writing MA course coming to a close, we cherish the stories we have told, but most importantly we cherish the stories we have created with each other.

We invite you to take a seat, and let us tell you a story.

Saahiti Shrikant, Eleni Socratous, and Will Triggs
Peninsula Editors-in-Chief

PENINSULA

With special thanks to Sam Riviere, Durham University, and Eggbox Publishing for making this possible,

to Paul Batchelor, Naomi Booth, Kayo Chingonyi, Claire Harman, and Sunjeev Sahota for their creative guidance and support,

and to Zsolt Balogh of Palma Studios for kindly allowing us to use a painted rendering of his inspiring artwork 'In Our Hearts Blind Hope' for our cover.

PENINSULA

PROSE

YUSUF CIMCOZ

Lully, Lulla

Wallace put his hands in his pockets, then quickly took them out of his pockets, then put them back in again as it was very cold, actually, then took them back out as it suddenly struck him as stupid to have his hands in his pockets when the weather was this bad and the bridge this icy, very dangerous, and then Tobi from the corner shop walked by and waved hello and Wallace couldn't help but imagine Tobi thinking, God, that Wallace fella's weird, constantly putting his hands in his pockets then taking them out like that, just decide, man. Then Wallace had to stop himself from looking back over his shoulder to see whether Tobi had put his hands back in his pockets. He also had to stop himself from going back and explaining to Tobi that no, he didn't regularly put his hands in his pockets and take them out so rapidly like that.

But he knew Tobi to be a very understanding young man. Only recently, when he had had to get feminine hygiene products for Ruby, bless her heart, she'd been dealing with a terrible bout of tonsillitis so couldn't get them herself, he had gone to the corner shop, the one by the football field, and explained to Tobi that he was needing to purchase some feminine hygiene products for the wife, you know how it is, and they had engaged in harmless banter for a bit, softly chuckling, until another customer had come in – a woman – and they quickly hushed themselves with awkward coughs. As he was about to leave, Tobi had smiled at him in a knowing way, in an acknowledging way, as if to say hey, that was a fun little conversation we had just then. And Wallace had smiled back before pushing the door open.

Now, of course, there was the risk that all of that had been for nothing. That Tobi now thought he had a weird mental thing about having his hands in his pockets or something. Maybe it made Tobi go over their previous conversation in a different light. Did Tobi now think that the humorous, inoffensive jokes that they had shared about feminine hygiene products had not been in good humour at all, that Wallace was not only a has-a-thing-about-hands person but also a kinda-creepy-around-women person? It didn't bear thinking about.

By the time Wallace finally plucked up the courage to discretely look over his shoulder Tobi had already turned a corner. He didn't think of himself as very anxious, no, Wallace considered himself to be careful, to be cautious, to be caring. He was a good dad, a good husband. He was the reason Ruby took her antibiotics every six hours as she should, he was the reason Robbie practiced his scales every day as he should. At some point, he had been imbued with this unfaltering internal clock, this wonderful machine that woke him up when he had to and made him go to bed when he had to and reminded him of his daily tasks and Ruby and Robbie's daily tasks and, to be honest, all his friends' and neighbours' tasks. Sure, sometimes, when Glen from the office made fun of his mismatched socks by the water cooler, for example – which had been a deliberate fashion choice that he and Ruby had mulled over for ages that was then never repeated – he thought of himself as a loser, but only sometimes, because then, when everyone else had forgotten, Wallace had been the only one in the office to get Glen a birthday present, and what did he get him? A pair of mismatched socks. Glen loved it. That was the kind of guy Wallace was. He spun things around, he made things better, he bounced back from things. All thanks to the clock.

The clock was telling him that Sewanee, Simon Sewanee, from 12b, had mysteriously skipped his regular evening walk today, or perhaps he had decided to take another route, because if he hadn't he would be running into him right about now.

"Wallace!" said Simon Sewanee from 12b.

He looked as though he had dressed in his appropriately-sized clothes early in the morning only to grow out of them throughout the day. It was evening now, so he was positively hulking in a tiny blue shirt and not weather appropriate tiny gym shorts. The wind swept his grey hair into a cowlick.

Simon speed-walked towards him. As he approached, Wallace considered the possibility of stopping for a chat. It was very cold. Surely Simon wanted to keep his temperature up. Ruby needed antibiotics before her inflated mutant tonsils blew her brains out.

Simon slowed his pace and reached for his earbuds.

"Can't chat," Wallace said and quickly swerved out of his way. "Sorry."

Simon gave him a strained grin, as if he was experiencing a sharp pain somewhere in his thin legs. He reaccelerated down towards the bridge.

Wallace wanted to kick himself. In the mouth. He would kick something more plausible if the road weren't so damn icy, even in his ridiculously expensive winter boots he was slipping and sliding all over the place, and now he would have to slip and slide all the way up the impossible incline he had the displeasure of calling his way back home, thinking about how miserable he is the whole way, how consistently shit, since what kind of forty-something balding man still gets nervous about a quick chat?

Despite himself, Wallace looked over his shoulder, maybe to see whether Simon had now stopped for a chat with Tobi, both of them now discussing how weird Wallace and his hands were.

Instead, he saw Simon slip and hit his head, very hard, on the tough concrete balustrade.

***

What a lucky guy he was! No, no, not a lucky guy, a skilled – no, a flirta – actually, just a lucky guy, maybe, but what luck! He'd been trying for ages now and finally, after weeks and weeks of trying to get in Eliza's pants – by god were those weeks toilsome, the long, elaborate messages – but finally the deed was done. Tobi was ecstatic. Positively beaming. She'd said it was good, too. He felt like a man, a sex mach – no, he just felt good, he felt good about himself. Very good.

Tobi wanted to follow up on this. This felt different. Eliza was cute, cuter than the usual suspects, and those usual suspects would all have to be blocked on their respective dating apps, obviously, because Eliza was the one, maybe. Not to jump the gun or anything, but she was really nice for a change, and her hair smelled so nice all the time, and she had so many different colourful scarves, and when she laughed it was an octave above her usual pitch. He'd have to tell dad to vacate the house for a subsequent date, sure to happen very soon, and maybe he could cook her something. Was he a good cook? No, but he was on the precipice now, the tipping point, one more solid date and they were in it for the long run, so tonight research would begin on the family computer. He wanted to try his hand at a hollandaise, that famously impressive-sounding mother of all sauces, but what did hollandaise go well with? Eggs Benedict? For a dinner date? It would have to be brunch. Maybe the hollandaise was a bad idea.

Someone shouted. Tobi stopped by the light and adjusted his beanie. Somewhere near the bridge. Another shout. Actually, on the bridge. Someone was on the bridge. And shouting. Really shouting. School kids, maybe? Tobi avoided them when he could, the little hooligans that hung out by the field and thumped their chests like gorillas whenever they managed to hit the shop windows with a ball. But this was a solitary scream, a man probably, shouting and shouting and shouting. For help. Someone needed help.

Tobi retraced his steps towards the bridge. Research would have to begin tomorrow.

***

If only he was the type of man to jump into action. No, Wallace was indecisiveness incarnate, the human equivalent of a house cat that claws and claws at the garden door with no intention of entering, a weasel of a man who would probably apologise if opportunity knocked him over the head. If only he knew first-aid. Of course he didn't know first-aid. He'd always hated biology, Ms. Dixon having been a notoriously tough grader, and now, years later, Wallace still cringed at the mention of blood. And there was blood, god was there blood, his face so red, and Simon was breathing so heavily, his chest moving up and down like that.

Wallace took his coat off – but the coat was too thick, surely, didn't they take their shirts off in the movies? – so Wallace took his sweater off, then he took his shirt off, and then he was left half nude in the unbelievable cold as he tried his best to put pressure on the wound. Why had no one heard him? He'd shouted so many times. He didn't know what to do, he so wished he knew what to do, and life was less than easy sometimes, it really was, those moments when the clock failed, and the clock really had failed this time, and the red stain was poking through the shirt now, how, how was there so much of it?

His heart was going. He needed to do his breathing exercises. He needed time to rub his hands against his temples and think about Robbie, his therapist had told him so, baby Robbie when he'd just been born, his sweet boy, bless his heart, but he also had to keep pressure on the head and so the hands stayed where they were, red now, as Wallace closed his eyes and counted to ten.

***

A murder.

Actually, no, the man with the thin ugly torso was Wallace, that harmless old fart, so Tobi picked up pace, carefully, sticking to one side of the bridge, the strong wind blowing into his coat. The guy on the ground looked worse for wear, and there was blood, but Tobi needed to get closer, and was that Simon? This would make a story, this would get Eliza excited, he'd tell her all about how he saved Simon Sewanee, the guy from 12b that does the evening walks, and then he'd get interviewed by a cute blonde news anchor in a jet-black pantsuit and wouldn't that make her jealous?

But Simon was dead. How could Wallace not see that? He was breathing, sure, but his head, the wound. Unresponsive. Tobi knelt down. He'd never seen someone die before. Mom had died in the hospital.

He felt like crying, suddenly. Wallace was crying. His eyes closed, shaking from the cold, counting to ten under his breath and starting over and over again, faster each time.

A week ago, Tobi had gone to a carol service with Eliza. He wasn't religious. But the choir had sung one he hadn't heard before, and he'd been moved to tears then, and then he'd shared his first kiss with her in the cold outside, dawdling afterwards, neither of them wanting to go back home.

He was rough on the words but the melody was there, so he started singing, softly, then just a little louder. He reached for Wallace.

Hand in hand, their breathing slowed, then Simon's chest stopped moving. But Tobi kept singing, over and over, until everything stood still in the cold dark night.

PENINSULA

JESSICA COOPER

Bad To See You

She sits beside me. I pull at the end of my sleeves. She moves closer. I stop. I move closer. She stops. We stare at each other for a moment. It is dark and it smells like spilt beer. I think of the stain on the carpet, how it sticks to my shoe. It is quiet. A car passes outside, and it backfires. She jumps a little, I jump a lot. We smile slightly. Her smile drags down in the corners. She relaxes into the seat, I follow.

I lean towards her, she moves away. She cries. I feel like I should say something. We sit in silence. I place my hand on her knee, she pulls away. We sit in silence for longer. You look fuckable when you cry, I say. She stands up and leaves. I follow half-heartedly. She closes the door.

I spend the night thinking about her. She does not message. I unlock my phone, I lock it again. I spend the next few minutes repeating this. I open our messages. I have sent three in an hour, she has sent none.

    Hello.
    That was fun.
    Did I make you cry?

I see her again the next week. She is crossing the

road outside the corner shop. I wave, she nods. We meet in the middle of the road. I go in for a hug, she slides past. A car brakes next to me and the driver swears. I tut and move out of the way. They wave their hand at me, I wave my fingers back. She stares at me from across the car roof, grimaces, and walks on.

Hello.

Later that week we are both at a party. Her friend has her arm wrapped up in hers. She does not notice me, her friend does, they walk outside as I enter the room. I nurse my drink and talk to someone I went to school with, I forget his name. He spends the time laughing at a girl stumbling upstairs. Typical, he says. I laugh and down my drink.

Good party.

***

Saturday night, a sticky nightclub floor. The second girl, tall and brunette, kisses me while dancing. I pull away for a moment to look at her. She is okay, perhaps a six. I lean back in. She pulls back laughing. I pull her against me. She twists a little then kisses me again.

I dance, she grinds. We kiss some more. A guy tries to cut in, I let him. He winks at me and I shrug back. I find the bar and order a drink, the brunette is beside me. I roll my eyes. I get out my phone. I take a photo with the girl, she smiles. I take a shot.

Hello *photo attached*

The message is sent. She is online, then she is not. I lock my phone and place it in my pocket. The Six is talking, I cannot hear her. It is loud in here, I say.

She leads me towards the toilets, walking ahead. I check my phone, the message has been read. I turn my phone off.

***

She is in the supermarket. She stands near the shampoo. I pretend to care about Aloe Vera gel. She looks at me, I look back. She reaches for Pantene. The shelf is too high. I offer to help by reaching for it. She stands back. I guess this is why your hair always smells so good, I say. She forces air out of her nose and walks away. I place the shampoo on the deodorant shelf.

You forgot your Pantene.

I hear her phone from across the shop.

Heard that!

She has switched her phone on silent.

Didn't hear that…

I flick to my shopping list and continue. Sweetcorn. Butter. I head towards the meat section. There are no reduced items, I will come back later. I add Pantene to the list.

I circle back, she is there. Reaching for the shampoo, I meet her hand. Thought I should try it, I laugh. She smiles and grabs the bottle before heading towards the checkout. I head to pay. Her basket is on the floor. She is gone. I buy a box of tissues, a grapefruit, and the Pantene. I forget about the reduced meat.

***

At home it is quiet. I think of her. Her hair, her smile, the way she shivers. I sit up in bed. I reset my cushions. The duvet pushed to the side. I hold my phone ahead of me. Her picture smiling at me. I click it off and back to the video. Back again and again. On and off. She smiles. They moan. I find myself smiling and moaning and smiling again. I land on her photo. I wipe the screen. It double clicks. I have liked her photo. It is dated three months ago.

I go to the bathroom and clean up. The extractor fan comes on with the light. The noise hurts. I turn the light off and continue in the dark. Throwing the toilet paper in the bowl, I flush.

My phone buzzes, a friend request. It is her friend.

Sending people to spy on me, huh?

I accept and scroll through her photos. Every other one contains her.

Heading to the kitchen, I like the most recent

photograph of them together and lock my phone. I put bread in the toaster and reach for the butter. I eat it over the counter. Crumbs fall on the floor. I brush them to the side with my foot. I drink from the tap and head back to bed.

***

I meet The Four in class. She needs a pen, I have a spare. My pen breaks five minutes later. I no longer have a spare. She laughs. I borrow a half-chewed pencil from someone, I forget their name. At the end of class, I throw the pencil in the bin with the pen.

Outside, she is smoking. Fancy one, she asks. I tell her I do not smoke. She offers again. I accept. I do not know how to smoke. A few shallow inhales later and I understand. We sit on a bench underneath a tree. She brushes her leg against mine. I brush back. She does not notice. I try again. She notices.

Fancy a drink, she says. I nod. We stub out our cigarettes and head for the bus. It is a long wait. I look at my watch, the timetable, my watch again. I step forward and look down the road, up the road, back down the road. She leans against the small seating area. She looks at her phone and messages someone. I read the name, John, with a heart emoji. She raises her eyebrows at me. No thanks, actually, I say.

We both get on the same bus. I climb on first. Prick, she says. I sit at the back. She sits ahead of me. A ladder shows on her tights, they climb her leg. Her skin looks soft.

I move and sit beside her again. This is our stop, I say.

We head into the pub and order.

***

The Four messages me. I turn my phone on silent. I watch the television and think about ordering food in. I scroll through social media. She messages again, I swipe the notification up. I lie down on the sofa. The cushions are hard. I reach down the side and pull out some coins. I find something plastic. I pull out a used condom. I throw it across the room and go to wash my hands.

> ~~Guess what I found.~~
> *You deleted this message.*

I open the messages from The Four. She wants to come over. I look around the house. I throw some boxers in the bottom of a cupboard. I tell her to come. A knock at the door. I scan the area one last time. I pick up the old condom and push it behind a curtain. I wipe my hand on my trousers.

A man is parked outside, he waves her goodbye, presumably John. I smile and raise a hand. He drives off. She invites herself in and looks around. She brushes her finger against the coffee table, collecting dust. She shrugs and sits down. Her face annoys me today. She is not as pretty, or smells as nice. I push myself against her and she kisses me. I think of someone else.

***

Another mutual friend's party. She is there alone this time. She does not leave the room when I enter. I stand beside her. She smiles and offers me a drink. She says she is hosting tonight. I nod and look at her lips as she talks. She covers her mouth as she laughs.

My phone buzzes, it is The Four. She raises an eyebrow and laughs again. The Four wants to know when we can meet again. I roll my eyes and block her number. I turn my phone off and put it in my back pocket. Other people have come and distracted her. I pull my phone back out and wait for the screen to load again.

The same old friend, I still cannot remember his name, comes over again. This time he is mocking the way the girls go to the toilet together. What would happen if they went alone? He laughs. I make a joke about breaking a nail on toilet paper, we sip at our drinks. His girlfriend comes over and strokes his arm. He grabs her and pushes her between us. My drink spills on my shirt. I wipe off the residue and scowl at him. Best go get that out, he says.

I do not know where the toilet is but I head upstairs. Couples crowd each step. I try to avoid touching them. Half-way up I knock one couple, their tongues choking each other as I push past. I groan. On the landing, it is quiet. She is stood waiting. This the toilet, I ask. She nods and pushes herself against the wall, arching her back. The door is locked, she says swaying before me. I try the handle, it opens. She laughs and falls into the doorway; her skirt rides up. She stands before me and lifts her skirt. I avert my eyes down but her skin looks soft so my gaze is dragged back. I lean against the door frame. She sits on the toilet and leans her head against the wall. She reaches for the toilet paper. Don't worry, I say, I've got it.

I think I recognise you from somewhere, she says.

***

I go home and make toast. I drink water before bed. She has not been online for a few hours, busy entertaining the remainder of the guests. I left early. The drink stained my shirt red.

Great night.
It was fun.

I listen to music that reminds me of her as I shower. Pantene smells good. The water is too hot, then too cold. I climb out and wrap myself in a towel. I leave the light off so the extractor fan won't start. The steam clouds the room.

Did you get home safe?
Is your head okay? You really smacked it off the bath.

My jeans are at the top of the laundry backet. I pull lace from the pocket. They still smell like her. I hold them to my nose, to my mouth. I wrap them around my fingers and brush them against my skin. I go to bed thumbing the edge.

***

I wake up. The house is quiet and my phone is on the floor. It is out of battery. I charge it as I grab breakfast. The screen lights up and she has not responded.

    Was it good for you?

    I distract myself with the news before heading to work.

    I price items behind the counter. I count each red tag. I put them down. I start again. My manager leans out of the break room door every twenty minutes. He scoffs under his breath but does not say anything. He smokes in there and does not move. Last month an inspector came in and saw. The inspector pointed their attention to the No Smoking sign before asking for a lighter.

    Her lace is in my pocket again. I touch it to check it has not fallen. A few times it has slipped. Did not know you were into that sort of thing, my manager laughs when it lands next to his boot. I place it back into my pocket. I return to counting.

    The bell on the door rings. She circles the aisles. She grabs some sanitary towels and heads towards me. I stand to greet her. The party was great, I say. She does not respond. I had a fun time, I say. I reach across the counter for her basket. My hand brushes hers. The lace is still wrapped around my fingers. She does not look at me but leaves her items on the counter. She walks out.

    Did I make you bleed?

PENINSULA

SAAHITI SHRIKANT

This Author Doesn't Know What To Title This Piece

Siri, how do I know if I am a good writer?

I'm sorry, I could not find anything for your search. Here are some articles I found on the web that could be relevant.

poem
/ˈpəʊɪm/

noun
1. a piece of writing in which the expression of feelings and ideas is given intensity by particular attention to diction (sometimes involving rhyme), rhythm, and imagery.

this is not what I asked for/ I know what a poem is/ at least/ I assume I do/ I'd be a shit poet if I didn't/ not that I'd remember anything once I'm eight drinks down/ also that's a bit biased/ I don't write poetry/ but go on/ show me what sells to the masses/ god forbid I write what I want to write about/ tell me/ what is it that sells/ who knows what I even write at this point/ might as well sell my soul for a profit/ is it a rhyme you want/ an overwhelming yet understated expression of feelings/ what feelings do you even expect from a seasoned professional like me/ do you mean to tell me that after years of subjecting myself to critical and commercial review I still own my feelings/ is that what you believe the creative life is, Siri/ did you think that's what it was/ cause I did/ I thought the words would just flow once I knew my purpose/ is this all I'm meant to do/ type word after word/ hope that someone will like it/ kill myself over it/ have you ever wondered why every writer is stereotyped as a drunk/ with a single malt whisky glass no less –

Finding articles for why writers tend to be more drunk and depressed than other professions.

Siri, are you fucking kidding me/ don't/ that is not what I asked for/ Siri/ stop —

<u>Top 8 Reasons why the writer in your life is probably depressed, survey finds —</u>
Have you ever walked in on your writer friend manically pacing around the room pulling at their hair muttering about writer's block and plot holes? Have you ever seen them write characters with traumas much too similar to theirs? Do they tend to constantly have a faraway look on their face? Do they seem more prone to worrying and overthinking —

…okay/ this is ridiculous/ I could've given you a better reason than that/ ABC's of advertising honestly/ a good hook line/ buzzwords/ relatability factor/ who's going to open that article with that terrible excerpt/ guaranteed it has a great clickbait title/ the millennials will love it/ no accounting for taste of course/ that's what they should have taught us in school/ how to write ditzy articles so that Buzzfeed pays my bills/ no/ of course not/ instead I was taught to rhyme/ and what meter is/ finding the appropriate word to sound just the right amount of pretentious/ what the correct usage of diction is/ what does it matter/ in a world where the attention is merely 7 seconds/ even you/ Siri/ an android designed

to accommodate my needs/ must I cater to you as well —

I am sorry. I was unable to understand what you said. Could you repeat it louder please?

why am I surprised/ but speaking louder is the one thing I cannot do/ lest they hang me for having an original thought/ one that wasn't cultivated for their pleasure/ even you Siri/ I must keep the button pressed at the right moments/ or you won't listen to a word I'm saying/ much less comprehend it/ sometimes it feels like no one listens/ no one speaks to me either/ not anything of worth anyway/ sometimes/ I think no one can/ is there anyone who is actually reading the words I'm bleeding through my skin/ or are they all just nodding their head politely in derision/ sometimes every interaction feels like one from a videogame/ press B to fast forward/ no words are of consequence when you skip through life mindlessly/ someone somewhere has the honor of being the lucky SOB/ that gets their personal language understood and reciprocated/ I wonder if anyone realizes that my personal language is hiding my secrets within my work in the hopes that maybe someday someone might see through them to me/ 8 reasons why a writer is depressed hah/ is that all they want/ this miserable occupation/ only fools choose this loneliness/ I am the biggest fool of them all/ Alex told me I'd regret it/ she was always so self-righteous about it/ no wonder she left me/ what was there to stay for/ except my wit of course/ then again/ my humor isn't for everyone/ I am a fool/ a willing one/ I'd rather be a fool than an ignorant dimwit/ belligerent/ that's what I am/ I should've thrown my manuscript down the drain while I could've/ it's too damn late now/ I have a voice now/ the truth is right there/ I just need to reach out/ they wouldn't understand/ to have a purpose like mine/ a purpose/ a passion/ to die for/ maybe that's why I'm so damn melancholic all the time/ hah/ there's a big word for you Siri/ get me its meaning/ I don't want to be —

This is what I could for the meaning of 'its'...

its
/ɪts/

determiner
1.   belonging to or associated with a thing previously mentioned or easily identified.

i.... this is exhausting/ I'm not sure why I'm even here/ talking to a system designed to overthrow humanity and make my job obsolete/ as if artificial intelligence could under the depths of human existence and experience/ poetry and fiction is more than technical sentences/ the truth is/ I have no reason to be miserable or petty/ or launch a manifesto against AI/ I wrote a book/ an entire book/ I birthed it from the tears in my body/ 600 pages heavy/ I got the euphoria when I held it in my arms for the first time/ I loved it/ no one would've loved it as much as I did/ that was its downfall/ I got the congratulations/ the banners and the posters/ the entire post publication malaise/ I won the lottery/ my child was beautiful and well-liked/ but my child was borne my misfortune too/ for it was always loved but never understood/ I suppose some things do run in the genetics/ they read it though/ they tried/ it was more than I had been afforded/ my family didn't understand/ then again/ why would they/ it's about them/ I didn't expect Alex to but I had hoped naively that Christian would've been able to/ she shares my genetics too/ don't siblings have a soul connection/ instead/ i watch the comments/ perhaps someone on the book tour might see through the lines/ do you know what a book tour is Siri/

Searching for what a book tour is —

Enough... no more searching/ I wish just for once/ I could have a real conversation/ there's nothing to search for/ there's no guidebook/ nobody to say for absolute/ is it a good thing I got a book tour deal/ there is no good or bad/ there is just the oppression of the industry/ art is long forgotten/ the ideal/ the good writing/ I am not a good writer/ I don't think I am/ now/ don't get me wrong/ I'm not a bad writer either/ I told you about the book tour/ didn't I/ I can't seem to remember most things nowadays/ it was a good tour/ crowded rooms/ superficial questions/ autographed books/ interviews/ the whole shebang/ I was lucky/ did all the m's/ saw every fucking m in the united states/ you name them I've been to them/ according to my publisher/ the millennials ate it/ that is the aim isn't it/ it was a great quirk to sell/ the writer who only sold his book in the m's/ the papers lapped it up/ made for a wonderful clickbait article/ we all know how well those sell/ an icon/ I'm not even famous/ god knows why I'd be/ my book is shit/ but my TikTok/ curtesy of an overpaid agent/ they're splendid/ Bukowski would bow down to my feet/ then get me drunk for selling my soul/ I'd prefer being drunk to this bullshit/ perhaps the stereotypes are not ill-founded/ 3 years Siri/ that's how long it took/ be a good writer/ they said/ speak your truth/ oh I spoke my truth/ but who was there to hear it/ the readers can sense whether you're being honest with them/ bullshit/ @unicorn421 on twitter seems to think my TikTok is better than my actual book/ what levels have I fallen to/ 3 fucking years/ Siri/ publicity is the win all be all/ @brandonlovesreading on Instagram thinks line 42 on page 80 is derivative and offensive to white liberals/ 3 years/ 2 deaths/ 1 divorce/ a book later/ I'm cancelled over one line/ I even went to all the m's Siri/ all of them/ Michigan/ Minnesota/ Missouri/ Montana/ Maryland/ Maine/ what's the last one/ goddamit/ note to self/ don't write a book while drunk/ hey Siri/ what's the long m state/

According to Wikipedia, the states that start with 'M' in the United States are:

Mississippi, Michi —

Mississippi/ that was it!/ I don't think I ever truly understood/ what it meant to be a writer/ what I was bargaining for/ I had simply had a dream/ a purpose I needed to fulfil/ and now that I am here/ this purpose feels empty/ or perhaps it's the road that I had to take/ I poured everything that I had into it/ just like they told me to/ I gave it my all/ do you think they can pick up on it Siri/ the disgust/ the shame/ the anger/ the sorrow in my throat/ is my audience really that smart/ would they be able to stomach my fear/ god knows I can't/ that's why I vomit it all over those pages/ would they recognize my mourning/ I have forgone my child to them/ they desecrate its grave with their ego critical reviews/ I am a mother/ and a mother needs to create/ I am burdened with the gift of creation/ of being a poet/ a writer/ lately all I seem to have is miscarriages/ I cannot afford to lose another child/ they wait/ eagerly/ for me to churn out next after next/ perhaps it could be worse/ I could be forgotten/ I should be grateful/ I am not/ I am disgusted/ I am furious/ with myself/ with them/ I am miserable/ happily so/ I have never before desired my own disgust so much/ I know no other way to be/ but I/ I miss it/ I miss writing/ for myself/ having it mean something/ Siri/ could you make one last search for me/

This is what I could find for your search: 10 ways to become a better writer, according to New York's pickiest book critics.

<u>Did you mean to search for: how to keep writing when you want to quit?</u>

ELENI SOCRATOUS

Gypsy Bird

Aunt Helena always skipped birthdays, school plays, and family gatherings. The only gathering she never missed was Christmas. Every year she wore the same pair of red boots with green bells on golden chains, and the permanent bounce in her step caused the bells to tinkle when she walked.

"Cheap," my grandma had called them once.

"I prefer the term vintage." Aunt Helena had winked at me.

Every Christmas I stood by the door, waiting to hear the familiar tapping of heels on our front porch. As soon as I opened the door, she knelt down and opened her arms wide.

"There's my favourite niece!"

"I'm your only niece Aunt Helena," I said between giggles as I launched myself at her.

She brought me dolls from Japan, dresses from Germany, and teddy bears from Serbia. After the unboxing, we sat together and she narrated her adventures to me. When my mum wasn't looking, Aunt Helena showed me her tattoos, one for every place she had visited. She described the waves she had surfed in Australia, or that one time when the car broke down in the middle of her safari tour in Tanzania. There was always a spark in her eye whenever she came back from a trip. Her hair always a different colour.

"It just seems more fitting to have blonde hair when surfing," she would say.

I just sat there, eyes wide, and listened to her narrate her life as if it was one out of a storybook. Her stories included all sorts of collections of people and descriptions of places I yearned to visit. And every year I asked her the same question, to bring me boots just like hers.

"So that we can be the same!"

"You don't want to be like me, how about a chocolate house from Sweden?"

But I did. I wanted to be just like her. When Aunt Helena entered a room, everyone turned to look at her; there was a confidence in her walk, her speech, her mere mannerisms. Bracelets dangled from her wrists, her hands always animated, trying to capture the passion that her voice carried. When she talked, others listened.

It became a tradition that after the Christmas holidays, my friends from school would gather around me, waiting to hear of Aunt Helena's gifts. No one's relatives could match up to her, with their nine-to-five office jobs and their occasional trips to the countryside. Aunt Helena was the cool aunt everyone wished they had and she was who I wanted to be when I grew up.

One of my favourite things when I was younger, was when Aunt Helena picked me up from school. Unlike my mum, she always got me ice cream from the van that was parked across the street.

"If Grandma asks why we're late, just tell her we went for a short drive, okay?"

I nodded and the two of us smiled at each other between licks of chocolate ice cream with sprinkles.

She never stayed long at my grandma's house after dropping me off – longer when my grandpa wasn't there. I assumed it was because Grandpa *really* disapproved of me eating ice cream before my meal. But every now and then, if my grandma insisted, Aunt Helena stayed for lunch. Those were the times when I first began to notice the little golden case she carried in her purse. Once we finished our food, she took out one small pill and swallowed it back with water. It was a weird movement, the way she drew her head back, with momentum.

"Can I try one?"

"No –"

"– No!" Aunt Helena and my grandma said at the same time.

She knelt down next to my chair and held the case close for me to see.

"These are to keep my nightmares away, Hailey. You don't have any nightmares, do you?"

I shook my head.

"Good."

Helena wasn't her real name. I know because a policeman stopped us once when she was doing 50 km/h in a 30 zone, and she had asked me to get her driving license out of her purse. On the plastic square, right next to her picture, it said the name Ellie Laher. That was when I realized my mum and her didn't share the same surname.

"You should make men work to say your name, Hailey," she said when I asked her about it. "Never let them give you nicknames. That's their ploy to make you feel small. You aren't small Hailey. Make them spend time on every syllable and drag out every sound. Your name should be a command. Besides, I don't look like an Ellie, do I?"

I nodded and drank in every word she said, like a bee bathing in honey. The question of the surname remained unanswered.

It wasn't until I asked my mum that I found out her and Aunt Helena didn't have the same dad. My mum sat me on the stool in our kitchen and told me the story of how my grandma was married to another man before – Aunt Helena's dad. One day, my grandma picked up five-year-old Helena and left their house. Two years later my grandma met my grandpa and a year after that my mum was born. My mum instructed me not to ask Aunt Helena nor grandma about it, but I was seven and the concept of two sisters having a different dad was newly discovered territory.

"Sometimes relationships just don't work out," my grandma said when I asked her. "And maybe that's for the best; if Helena's dad and I hadn't separated, then I wouldn't have met your grandpa, and I wouldn't have you or your mum."

She poked my stomach and pulled me close for a

hug. I never asked about him again. Never asked about whether he kept in touch with Aunt Helena or if he had another family.

When my first boyfriend cheated on me, Aunt Helena was the one I turned to. Looking back now, I hardly remember his face, let alone the sound of his voice, but I was fifteen and my heart was shattered. I called her crying while in school and in between shallow breaths I told her that I had caught him kissing another girl in the toilets.

"He said that I was ugly and boring and that he wants someone who will give him a blow-job when he asks for one."

"That fucking asshole. I'm on my way."

We went for ice cream, only this time the ice cream van wouldn't cut it. Parked in the McDonald's parking lot, she wiped my face using her lavender wet wipes and told me that no man deserved my tears.

"Never trust men, Hailey, and don't allow anyone to touch you if you don't want them to."

We dipped fries in strawberry milkshakes, ate chicken nuggets, and Big Macs and at the end, right before leaving, we each got a Smarties McFlurry. Her red lipstick left marks on her spoon and straw.

"How come I've never seen you with someone?" I asked her in between spoonfuls of ice cream.

She furrowed her brows together. They were bleached into a platinum blonde to match her hair, but dark brown had begun to show – loose reminders of who she was beneath the dye.

"There have been some men, but I don't know."

She seemed like she was going to say more but then she pursed her lips, twirling the white cream in her cup in search for Smarties.

"Don't you ever, I don't know, want to have a family? I wouldn't say no to a cousin."

There was the case again, the gold one. She took one pill out and after a slight pause picked out a second one. Throughout the years I began to associate the golden case with her, an extension of her arm. There was a pattern to it. The case was invisible when she first returned from a trip, but as the days went by and her hairline returned to its natural colour, the case appeared more frequently and the pills increased in quantity. Before we knew it, off she was again in search of her new adventure.

She washed the pills down with water and then resumed eating her ice cream.

"That type of lifestyle works for your mum, and maybe one day for you too," she turned to me and smiled. "But I don't think that's the lifestyle for me. I am a, what do you call it, a gypsy bird."

"You mean a gypsy heart?"

She raised an eyebrow in question.

"Well, it's either a gypsy heart or free as a bird."

"Potatoe, potato. You know what I mean."

Afterwards, we went to the cinema and Aunt Helena picked the least romantic movie. There was action and blood and war and everything I needed. She held my hand throughout and never stopped teasing me by trying to steal my popcorn.

There isn't a specific moment that highlighted our drifting apart. With the start of my university degree, it was me who began to skip family gatherings. That was around the same time when Aunt Helena's biological father had reached out to her. Turns out he had married again and Aunt Helena had another sister. A sister who was now getting married and had invited Aunt Helena to the wedding. My mum told me she found the invitation in the bin at my grandparents' house.

She never called. I sometimes did. As the gulf between us grew, so did the pessimistic note in her voice and her concern that men would lure me into their trap, that I shouldn't confine myself to an office job and had I considered taking a gap year?

"Men only want certain things from you, Hailey. Don't fall for their games. Also check out this volunteering summer project in Crete that I sent you, it's got to do with sea turtles and everything."

"They're not all bad. I've actually met some very nice guys here at uni." I seasoned my comments with the occasional lighthearted laugh and made sure to tell her I would check the link later.

Whereas before I couldn't get enough of her, now I kept our phone calls short. We stuck to basics and after the pause on both ends went on for too long, I said I needed to finish my coursework. I didn't want to only see the world through Aunt Helena's eyes. I wanted to touch and be touched by men, to kiss and be kissed. I wanted to do an internship at a law firm in the summer. I wanted something that she didn't approve of and I didn't know how to talk to her about it.

At dinner tables I listened to her talk, but now my eyes were not just glued on her. I noticed how my mum was cut off; a joke left unfinished; a story barely started. How my grandma laughed a bit too hard and how my dad shifted in his seat whenever the preaching on "men are trash" began. My grandpa would ask Helena to go slow on the wine, joking that there wouldn't be enough for the rest of us. She brought the glass to her lips and downed the liquid inside. She talked politics and demanded attention and agreement on her opinions. I stuffed my mouth with mashed potato, swallowing down my arguments. And there was the case. Little round pebbles washed down with wine while everyone else was tidying up.

The first boyfriend I took home was a course mate of mine from university. He was from Greece and as he couldn't fly home for Christmas, I invited him to spend the holidays with my family.

The familiar dangling of bells and that deep laugh crashed into the house the moment my dad opened the door. I wiped my palms on my jeans and walked towards the living room with Panos following close behind me.

"There's my favourite niece!" she said and pulled me in for a hug.

"Aunt Helena, I would like you to meet Panos."

"It's a pleasure to meet you, Hails has told me so much about you," he said.

Her smile fell. Not by a lot, no, barely at all. It became forced, strained. I often question whether that was the moment when she knew, when we both knew, that she and I weren't that similar after all. While she dragged out the syllables and demanded respect for her name, in her eyes I was being made smaller. I was 'Hails' now, and I allowed it.

A month before I graduated, Aunt Helena took her life. My mum asked if I wanted to talk about it, but it was me who held her up when she cried over the coffin.

The funeral didn't last long. I stood last in line, right next to the open casket, and shook people's hands when they gave their condolences. Most of them were my grandparents or parents' friends. I know because every single face was familiar. I wondered if any of her friends knew.

There was only one man I didn't recognize. A man who grabbed my grandma's hand and shook it, both their knuckles turning white as they held on to each other, lips quivering.

"Goodbye Ellie-Bear," I heard him whisper when he leaned over the casket.

I turned to look at him but he was already walking in the opposite direction. There was no mistake; the walk with just enough bounce in each step was the very same. That was the only time I allowed myself to look at the unsmiling figure lying next to me. Brown soft curls framed her face. Long gone was Helena with her loud voice and louder personality. In that moment, she was just Ellie.

PENINSULA

WILLIAM WOODGATE

The Wistful Disappearance of Summer

I first met Amy back in February, at some quiet party. I was there through invitation of an old school friend, who, like me, had moved recently to the city. The party took place in some small, scarcely dressed flat, dotted in ornaments of the 'moment.' The floor was cheap linoleum and upon it danced a wealth of people who spoke freely of some indistinct and ever elusive 'greatest' art. No artist was ever settled on, but several hometowns from which an array of artists could have originated were shared like business cards or evidence of some much greater, although never exhibited, mound of knowledge. Everyone was smart because everyone allowed for everyone to be smart, and any whim of stupidity, in whatever form it may have appeared, was so obviously ironic that to question a person's opinion was an act of satirical genius.

Amy was midway through mistaking Sandberg for Ginsberg when I first approached. She held a non-distinct spirit in her hand, mixed with two dashes of lime. I said something about fog and cat's feet, and she smiled, rattling her brain for something to say. Before long she was talking about her art, something vague about taking it seriously. I tried to engage her in an earnest way, but apparently I just didn't get it. It's because you're from a big city, she smiled, artists are more like me, from small towns far away. I didn't say anything, and I don't think she wanted me to. She liked it when her words were left to linger, as if they all meant something.

The night dripped onward. I learnt she was a sixties girl, and fell in love with her voice. She wore the type of jeans most commonly found on pinup posters of hippies stood in overgrown fields. I told her it was strange how some decades seemed to go on forever, but she pretended to not understand. Almost immediately upon our meeting, the decade became immutable in my vision of her. She was, in many ways, a better depiction of the era than any poster could ever have been. For some reason, I think she would've disliked that. I thought about telling her how it was odd that the past never seemed static, and was always open to perennial redefinition, but decided against it. Instead, I mentioned some of my poems, and she found a delicate way to circle back to her art.

We stayed within each other's words until the party reached its zenith, when we decided to loudly, although to no one in particular, announce our departure. We headed not far from the flat, out onto the cold and empty beach. We took off our shoes and socks, letting the soft sand sprinkle over our itching feet. I complained about the long winter, and professed a new found admiration for spring. She laughed and mentioned something about seasons flowing like oceans into other oceans, and I looked far into the Gulf of the Farallones, pretending to see where the water moved into the Pacific. She smiled and said it didn't work like that.

We became entangled after that night. And spent

the following morning chasing the buzz toward LA. I was surprised to learn that Amy came from a prominent family, and the presumed importance of her surname was as good as money. To my benefit, she made good of this privilege to spend it liberally in the ritzy parts of town where such frivolous features demanded attention. She had a thorough education too, and so was afforded the satisfaction to speak perfectly well about anything of little importance.

    We stirred through the city until early summer. I became enthralled by the ocean, the sand that ran beside it, and the people who spent each day sat opposed the sun, burning. I was living a life I was unaccustomed to, and soon came to understand a few things. Everyone was a struggling artist of some sort, and the greater their struggle the artier they were. Reading poetry was of little importance, good poems were born from experience, and bad poems could be blamed on the weather. We met a girl one night who explained this all self-evidently. She liked to sit back in men's shoes and speak in a deep voice as if she had it all figured out. She said I was self-conscious because cancer was in retrograde.

    All of our nights started the same way. We drove through the city in Amy's car, hunting for hard-to-come-by and quiet streets to race down. The air above the buildings cooled and the day's heat would begin its slow ascent, the humidity drowned all sound, and once the eastern mountaintops surpassed the sun's brow all things flourished a little differently. People die to be on nights like this, she once said, and I let her words float until she continued, and sometimes nights like this kill them. The streets blossomed with an erotic glow and waves of natural light become tangled between the emptying buildings. I always found about these moments, no matter how many times I experienced them, that I was vulnerable to slight tinges of disassociation, as if we drove through a photo album, or inhabited a city of cut-outs. But I always snapped out of this pretty quickly, as I watched the shadows flicker beneath the moving cars and took comfort in the whispers of day and night.

One night we went to a party hosted by an old college friend of mine. He was celebrating something significant and it made me uneasy. I was in my mid-twenties, and on occasion stuttered with the idea that I should have more to show for it. He had a small, all-white apartment stacked atop an old renovated office-block. We met a girl there who Amy knew. Her name was Grace, and she had a habit of tapping the side of her nose, and whenever she did it would twitch like an engine started. They talked for a while and I spoke to her boyfriend. Everyone called him Tally because he liked to stand to the side of the party and count whoever was in the room. I liked him because he had an effortless way of taking in the spirit of place without allowing for himself to be taken over. He asked me questions about my poetry and I struggled to remember anything he said. We spoke for some time until Amy dragged me away.

He's a bore, don't you think? Oh, I don't know, I told her. She sipped from a little cup of vodka and chewed on the bitter ice. She was wearing a red summer dress with white stripes across the top, because it made her feel like the American flag. He's too postmodern, she went on, he thinks the world is there to be mapped out and he's too afraid to get lost.

    We stayed and drank for another hour or so. There was a man who no one knew wandering around taking photos and we posed a few beneath the window arch. And then Amy asked for one more and wanted me to remove myself, so that she could be alone and pout and be borne before the bright moonlight. I remember one evening, when were alone along the pier, her fathered called and joked of her being an heiress. I smiled and nodded and she acted as though she were disinterested, but she cherished more than any other her tendency to act in the dramatic vein of certain aristocratic socialites, and would often do the sort of things I imagine she believed heiresses should do, like brood beneath a darkening sky and be lonely in front of cameras.

    We left the apartment before the party was over and headed out onto the cooling streets. Amy wanted to find a little club called LaCie's. We had been there once before and had a horrid time. It was an eye-sore with daring red canopies and round bouncers that wore jackets they couldn't afford. It was the sort of place that was nice until everyone knew it was nice, and in consequence came to be frequented by the sort of morally suspicious men who were forever stranded in the trail of a culture they desperately clawed at. It's often presumed that such men are tough or hardened, but they are only aggressive. They struggle with the ultimate dilemma, a total disconnect between who they perceive themselves to be, and how they are received by others. As if their entire existence is a series of pleading letters written in a language that no one can understand. Amy used to like to stand at their side and watch them argue and fight. On one occasion they took offence to her watching and began to shout obscenities in her direction. Just ignore them, she said, that's the best thing about other people, when you close your eyes they stop existing.

Our hunt for LaCie's stopped when we stumbled upon Amy's car. She wanted to head out and drive anywhere, and I thought it was a good idea. She was much drunker than me, so I got behind the wheel. We moved out to wherever we thought the ocean was, spotted it by luck and made haste. It was camouflaged at the horizon in a mix of unwavering black and the darkest blue I'd ever seen. Even in the dead of night there was no escaping the traffic. She angled her body so that her legs stayed straight and her shoulders peered out over the open road, letting her hair paint the side of the car and looking ahead just enough so that the quick air didn't hurt her eyes. I tried to leave the city by following the coast, but it appeared immeasurably. I squinted my eyes to keep the road lines in definition, as Amy sang over the radio, letting her voice flitter in the drag of the car.

She told me about some fancy sounding art expo being held in New York, sometime during the winter. She thought she had a chance of getting her work on display if she showed up and was herself in front of people who mattered. I pulled over in a lay-by pressed to the side of a shallow cliff, which jutted out from the road and pointed off into the dark. Beneath, the sound of restless pebbles getting pulled by the sea bounced off the rocks. I wiped my eyes and felt regret about having driven. We left the car and went to sit on the roadside barrier.

There was no light where we were, only the outlying buzz of the city, which hovered above the mountains like translucent cloth. There were no stars either, except for the ones over the ocean and the same ones again rippling on the ocean-top. I thought from where we were, watching the water flow into the sky, that I could see the finest of white lines, as if the horizon were an opening eye. Amy pointed to a small opening of jagged sand that turned to slimy rock and stretched out like a natural pier. She wanted to head down and I followed.

The cliff appeared more treacherous when it rose above us, and suddenly the restless pebbles were agitated and unwilling. She held the lower seam of her dress and raised her arm until she looked like a petal, the rest of the fabric sticking to her body as the wind grew and grew, and for the last time I held her, softly and unknowing, and she spun away like a ballerina. Take a picture of me. I don't have a camera, I told her. Then pretend. And she headed out toward the end of the miniature peninsula, taking her final steps as if she glided across a catwalk. I noticed that, from where I stood, only ten or so feet from the peninsula's beginning, that the water no longer rolled to its break, but was instead interrupted by fearsome and lofty rock. I looked over to Amy, who in my drunken vision, posed against a lucent moon. The beam of which spread the Pacific and reached its narrow end at the peninsula's tip, as if Amy stood atop a polished tree of ashen light. She became a silhouette; a happy, dancing shadow backdropped against the black sea. I could faintly hear her shouting as she began to dance, and so I imitated the taking of pictures, watching the water flick up around her. Each drop seemed to bring her to life; each drop vanishing as it appeared; each drop as bright as the other, flickering in the darkness, seemingly at random, and then without warning, all flickering at once.

I stood frozen and shackled, and decry to this day, to whomever that asks, that they never found the body. But in truth, when they did, it was so bloated and un-Amy-like that I know she would've preferred for people to think that she was forever lost at sea.

I felt desperate and lonely after that night, and so moved back to my parents and tried to recapture my spirit. In those empty months I felt as though I was waiting for the world to end, knowing that it never would. Eventually I gathered enough of myself and headed to New York with whatever of Amy's artwork I had in my possession. I went to the expo and showed whatever I could to whoever would spare me the time. At first, there was no person that offered more than a passing glance, until I mentioned how the artist drowned in the pitch-black sea, and then in an instant her work became imbued with such elusive properties that they could never be achieved by the living. Immediately, the newfound attention was outpouring and overwhelming, it became sticky and repulsive, and I scurried out of the building, shaking their gaze off my arms as I left. I went and stood along the Hudson River line and watched the water move into the bay. I thought back to the first night we met. How we walked down the beach and found a pier that stretched into Drake's Bay. We dangled our legs over the edge and thought LA would be a nice change. I told her how there was something I quite enjoyed about watching the emptying offices fade off into the night, and she told me that would make a beautiful poem. She poured cheap spirits into cheaper cups and traced the night with a hazing finger, formed a gun with her hand and shot the moon over the distant Earth.

Now, I'm stood alone in New York City, stuck alongside inky water, clenching my eyes so I can see her again. That's the tragic thing about memories, if you're not careful they move into one another like crashing waves, and all you can do is hope you don't get lost in the wake.

PENINSULA

POETRY

CATRIONA INGLIS

Imago Dei

My body is a temple it tastes of
sacrifice; citrus scented perfume pools
in the dip of my collarbone above

where the line of worshippers kneel at my
feet, stethoscopes adorning their necks like
Pellegrina. In return I comply;

and their demands fall like prayers on my ears;
and I offer blood as an answer to
too many questions, to wipe away fear

like a bandage on a reopened scar.
Because my body is a temple it
smells like rain in autumn, shines like bright stars

when I trace the curve of my spine with hushed
fingertips to ease out pain, it delights
in the release my palm offers: untouched

by antiseptic and narcotics. Since
my body is a temple it can be
entered at a whim; no need to convince

me I acquiesce to all communion
that I swallow daily from the bottle
you prescribe. Confess to me in human

apology your diagnosis it
cannot hurt me anymore because my
body is a temple and I admit

I know all the hymns it sings when it screams.
My body is a temple it has to
be true, as no other truth could redeem

this worship, delivered from joy, transfused
whole. But this creed has no prognosis that
can escape its writ of glory; left bruised

through prayer; carved in flesh and love-broken.

Asthma Attack prelude in C major.

Let me tell you a song to which I know all the words
25 stiches from wrist to thumb
the colour of the thread has me thinking of blood oranges
and the remembrance of snow
the tune idles at crochet pace
float me a minim

Stiches replaced by Hairline Fracture
she whines up the octave
I harmonise her F# with a root G
I watched my first ice hockey game on another G day
Number 6 got his stick caught
it cracked against ice thicker than all the partings in the room
you'll need a clacker for the snap

Hairline is followed by Four Adults And A Trolley
the quavers of their feet clash in angles
against the dissonance of their voices
I transpose to tune out the hand they clutch
melting ice like oranges, that spills in tracks of wheels
one bar and they're gone

Enter the scherzo in D♭
Chest Pain fights against the white light
of the bulb bright against his bald head
Abdominal Pain sings her own songs in Fs and Cs
I don't know the words but the tune is shrinking balloons
Nose Bleed wails in segments against tears
Another enters Another leaves

Caesura.

My breaths like squeaking tires against new tarmac;
the need for quavers, overrun with semibreves
as oxygen is coaxed in like moths
the light not bright enough
the rubber expands, crackles against hairs I hear them
snap

Crescendo!

a doctor sings arpeggios in my ear, the timpani play the
beating
of my heart the colour of oranges
hockey cracks over and over against the ice
that clouds vision on a breeze

No. 12 Eastacre Road.

9:01am

I am at war with a rat in the yard outside my house. His name is Oscar, after the fake boyfriend I used to call when I walked home alone late at night. Each day he comes to check the rubbish bins that adorn my house, each day he finds them empty. I smile vindictively at him, I have won again. Yet each day he returns, he does not know yet that hope is futile. I watch him through breath-smudged windows, I wait for his scuttle, his furtive glance, the nose scratch that always gives him away. I shall not let him win. I hoard rubbish bags like bullet shells, I fill my house with them, yet still he comes.

10:12am

I have befriended a pigeon who likes to visit the apple tree whose branches reach for the edge of my bathroom window. Her name is Cleopatra after a girl I knew at primary school who collected the wax of baby bells in one thick ball. By the end of the year the ball was so big she did not have room in her bookbag for her writing homework. She got detention for three days. I always tidy up for her visit, Cleopatra is a haughty pigeon, I run my hands along my kitchen counters to collect the crumbs I offer her. Sometimes my offering is too small and she looks away, her head lifted in royal annoyance. I ran out of bread three days ago but I still find the crumbs, stashed between doorframes, under tissue boxes and discarded papers. I try to be a good host.

11:27am

There is a speckled brown and grey cat that patrols the perimeter of my house. His face is caved in slightly as if he once withstood a powerful blow, so I know he takes his job very seriously. His name is Vimes after a neighbour I once had who liked to mow his 6 square foot patch of lawn at sunrise each day so that he always knew when the boy who delivered the newspapers was late. Sometimes I hear him at the door and know it is time for an inspection. I always let him in; it would not do to upset the watch. He comes in, shoulders hunched, paws tentative, eyes slanted to take in the faded red of the carpet that lines my stairs, he sniffs the air, once, twice. Once I tried to tip him with the last remnants of the previous week's milk but Vimes is an honest cat and refused the bribe.

12:42pm

My neighbours have a small pond. I watched them build it several months ago, he dug the ditch himself and I saw him transition from excitement to disillusionment in a matter of hours, digging is always harder work than you expect, I've read Holes. She would come out every now and again and coo encouragement. They lined the bottom of the hole with bin bags and old tarp, sunk in the plastic bowl, I watched her bring round the garden hose to fill it. A few days later she came back with pot plants, rustically calved stones and pebbles and a small solar panelled fountain. She fussed around the pond for days trying to fit it into the shape of her yellow lawn. The couple spent the next few weeks sporadically visiting the area to nod at one another but before a month they stopped. They were replaced by a new couple named Frederick and Velma after friends of my parents who smelled faintly of musty cinnamon and once invited us over to give a 3-hour presentation on their holiday in the Swiss Alps. I prefer Frederick and Velma, I am hoping for tadpoles in the spring.

2:05pm

I am experiencing a small invasion. Small in size but large in quantity. An ant colony that previously commanded the territory surrounding my compost bin has clearly grown impatient and has come to claim the tithes I have been neglecting to pay. Ants are rather difficult to distinguish so they are all called Reginald after my year 6 piano teacher who used to line buttons along the white keys to reward me for perfect scales. The first Reginald through the gap, the small hole they've drilled in the wall below my kitchen window, is a buff, warrior looking kind of fellow. He leads the charge towards the small piece of tinned sweetcorn I've left out as tribute. A whole line of Reginalds dash for the corn, buff Reginald reaches it first and, holding it aloft in triumph, runs it back through the no man's land and out of sight. I get up from my place on the floor to lay a circle of salt around the retreating ants. They are satisfied for now but give them an inch…

6:27pm

The afternoons hang long without company but I like to watch the fall of the sun in anticipation. She, comes, at last. Her name is Maria. I see her green eyes glow through the hole in my fence I leave open for her and catch a glimpse of russet fur through the circle I've polished in the misted window. I press my face against the cold glass, holding my breath to keep it transparent. Maria shuffles closer, so I can see the white of her chest, the black of her nose. She looks thinner than yesterday. Another pair of green eyes appear then just behind her, they are smaller, closer to the grass. "Ah," I breathe, "an introduction is in order." My words cloud them from view and I huff in annoyance trying to use the sleeve of my cardigan to wipe away the fog but when I look again Maria is gone. I rush to the back door, fingers hover over the door knob before I shakily open it. I line up the tips of my toes with the edge of the room to squint into the dark but Maria is gone. I will have to ask her daughter's name tomorrow.

10:16am

Oscar didn't come this morning. I suppose I won.

KATE MARSHALL

Jellyfish in the Sky
Arnhem, Holland.
September 17th 1944.

Through the gap in the curtains
    I can see them,
        floating down.
            They seem friendly
                and soft
                      like snowflakes.
                I want to tell mumma about them
            but I know she shuts the curtains.
        So I won't.
I watch them.
        Sometimes they fall very slow,
            other times they swing from side to side.

            I don't like the sharks.
                They are at the top of the sky.
                  They move behind
                        the clouds
                and they are scary.
            But they make the jellyfish,
        so I trust them.
    I like to think of the jellyfish
as my friends,
        they are here to protect the houses
             in case the sharks swoop
                down
                    to hurt us.
                    I wonder if everyone
                      can see them

or is it just me.

I think mumma must not
see them,
she does not like the outside world.
And she never believes me when
I tell her.
I told her
the jellyfish had little legs
hanging down at the bottom.

Maybe
they are here
to tell me good things.
They have never been here before.
They might be here to tell us about papa.
Where he is
When he's coming home
He is in the sky too

Maybe they saw him.

The jellyfish have all disappeared now.
There are loud noises
and mumma has
put us under the table.
I don't know why.
Mumma says I should not ask so many questions.
She says we are hiding but
the best hiding place in the house is
in the linen basket.

I think mumma is afraid
of the jellyfish.
I am not afraid of them.
I am afraid that papa will not
come home.
And that no one will ever believe
me.

Papa saw it
    I know that he would
        like the jellyfish.

        I want to write him
                another letter telling him all about them,
        I will tell him as well that he said
      he would come to my birthday
    when I turn 7
and that is in two weeks and one day now.

    I will add a drawing of the jellyfish,
        he says I am the best drawer he has ever seen.
              Sometimes I get letters from him.
              But they are all the same,

"I will be back soon. I love you and your mother very much."

            I think mumma is writing them.

David,

1.
>it rips out
>from underneath me
>what was normal?
>scream
>scream until it comes back

2.
>without a knowing goodbye
>i refute it
>i renounce it
>i declare it, wrong
>am i mad?
>no, it will leave soon

3.
>to bribe you with
>and grasp it
>i can reach it
>simply tug at me
>if you just tug at me
>you'll see what i have left
>what we can hold onto
>i can surrender!
>and you can sacrifice
>we can arrange all of this

4.
>a dead stomach of regret
>scoop me out
>these curdling organs

study their mould and decay
peel back the skin to see the sorrow

5.

crack
fairness is a myth
deserving something, as just
that high pitched ringing
gets louder, and sharp

6.

each day
the low hum
vapour noise
inject reality
into those warm veins
things
saying things
doing things
survival of the old
and dissatisfactions

7.

altered
calm and
closer
i feel heavier
full up of
what it was like to be
without, and
nod
golden foil, crimpled and creased
a faded glow, glimmers in the heat.

III. I Only Have To

for when I miss you, and you're not there
and I crave some form of connection
I only have to bite my lip
and I remember you
chewing the coating off a chocolate bar
listening to the crinkle of the foil
focusing on your tongue
and teeth.

I drive
and scream myself hoarse
only you come to mind when I close
my throat
to cry.
I retch
and I can feel your hand
warm, on my back
telling me how strong
I am
how I should get some sleep.

you're in every vacant stare
you become every person I kiss
and you're here

in this room, sitting
quietly
on sleepless nights
so, when I miss you, and you're not there
and I crave some form of connection
I only have to say your name and close my eyes
and you come back to me.

JOANNA MORTON

Summer Heat Spells

Sepia stained
Glass windows
Wavering, left
In limbo

Disorderly, pipe
Cleaner tibia
Knocking, almond
Eyes rolling

Dandruff caught
On striped,
Rolled doormat
Barred from home.

Poor little bumble
Where you been?
Come sit here,
Get buzzed with me.

Patches

Scuff the rough
With sandpaper
Blur the edge
Smear over the mould
That torn glaring
Hole
Was never there

Pewter paint
Flat matte
Works for a while
But in a few weeks
There are a few tiny cracks
And a few dark marks
Coming back.

Grab the roller
Splotch the stains
All over again
Prod the brush
So it dapples
And blends
Over a bulge

That grows and
Stands as an
Interior design tumour
Protruding an inch
Away from the wall
But it's fine it
Blends it blends.

Thankfully You Were Too High to Remember This

You were cut apart with scalpels, knives and saws
And pieced back together with bolts and screws,
Two titanium rods managed to meld machine
And man, then over metal and bone, your skin
Was stretched and stitched up with a seamstress's needle,
Concealing the back-breaking work with a bow.
When we eventually got to
ICU I'd never seen you look so
Pale and fragile, as if they'd accidentally
Injected china into your bones instead.
You were frozen, staring at the ceiling
Transforming fluorescent bulbs into stars
You tried to smile as we hovered,
Floating in your spiral galaxy. The nurse arrived.
Checked monitors and moved the bed back up,
Saying how you must want to see us.
It was instantaneous, you started
Grimacing, gasping with the little energy
You had left. I tried to come to your aid:
'He doesn't like that,' I said, 'put it back'
No one noticed the girl in the corner,
Or your agony. The nurse left. You clawed the sheets.
I tried to hang on to the wall, but it breathed,
It ballooned and shrunk away from me,
Too slippery smooth to grab. The world swayed.
Losing balance and self-respect
My body hit the floor. The nurse came back.

Sommarøy

I'll harpoon a chunk out of the universe,
Then swallow a black hole
Let the fireflies burn my throat
And roll the dense marbles on my tongue.

My freckles will merge
To your constellation,
So the one you look for at night
Will be me.

Maybe two empties fill a whole
Void that a full life cannot satiate,
But this will satisfy.
Been too busy looking at the next page,

Skipping forward to fill yourself with dread
With things that keep
You awake in bed. Wasting
When you could be dreaming

Of ice strong enough to encase
Sun and moon from a frost-bitten comet
That is hungry for change
And this difference is that things stay the same.

Present never did exist, now
We drift through space
At no identifiable pace.
No one has the right amount

And bemoans they didn't
Spend it well enough,
But who's trying to sell?
I can't afford these rates,

So I'll make it stop.
I won't just give you the world,
I'll give you all the time in it
I'll give you the lot.

Ode to 'In Our Hearts Blind Hope'

The cosmos
Drops
Onto Durham Cathedral,
Spires inhaling stars.

Bodies of indigo
Silently play
Musical statues
Minds jointly transfixed.

Faces bloom under
Countless candlelight
Running like wax
Up the central tower

Shades pulsing through
Kaleidoscopic frame,
A glacier rush spikes down,
Icy arms reaching

Out to buttresses.
Flames flaring
Into butterflies,
Building to rush

With the crescendo
Of violins
Growing, until
The pastoral glitch.

Crack and crackling
Ascending embers,
A spark of life
Defining structures.

Glitter rain sunbeams
Dripping gold elixir glory
Leave us in the lustre
Of a fresh dawn.

The glow seeps into shadows
As do the people,
Their steps
A little lighter.

Always the Hardest

The words ran around on my tongue.
They played hooky and
Murdered in the dark
All in the cage of my teeth.
Some slipped down into my
Stomach, and gurgled. I hoped the
Acid would dilute the rancid taste,
Sterilise the pathogens of pathetic psych-
So that it came out clean
And numb.

No!
Not yet, I'm not ready yet.
I know it will
Help!
Can't you read it in my eyes?
Hear it escape from closed lips
Save me!
The cocoon is now ravaged,
A crumpled ghost of its former self.
Fire!
Burn what's left and let grass grow.

Don't make me bring up that old
Corpse, that skins me alive

From inside out, on its assent.
I had only just pat earth on its limbs.
Please!
Don't wake it. Don't make it speak.

Re-lease Me

A man put a 'To Let' sign up
Outside my house the other day.
I listened to the whirring of screws
Then he picked it up and took it away.
Despite installing and unnerving me
It turned out I didn't need to stress
With worries of immediate eviction,
He'd got the wrong address.
The endless uncertainty of
Living in a house that is a home
But not my own

Where I cannot make
A hole in
One more brick in the wall.

To decorate and hang sleek frames that hold
Poetic art, or ornate mirrors that double the
Room. I can see a duplicate me, smiling
From the spectral glass, on the wall. She can
Host a sesh, have a pet, a pet! A little scamp to call
My own. A domesticated wolf or an adorably arsey cat.
A rabbit, guinea pig, hamster, mouse, lizard, snake, rat.
Anything. Please, can I just have a pet?

There are too many that have no home of their
Own. My walls may be naked
Under a clinical glare yet even half of one
Is better than none.
I might be happy if
I didn't have to powder my cheeks pink

To cancel the pugnacious green
When another friend tells me they
'Can't believe we just bought a two-bed house!'
(Puppy may or may not be included).

It will be years (decades?) before I can dare to
Scheme of a scam reliable enough
To pay a mortgage, let alone a down payment.
So, I live,
With the discomfort of routine inspections,
A stranger walking into
My sanctuary uninvited

To check I have not made
A hole in
One more brick in the wall.

WILL TRIGGS

As the trail ends

Stoured in seaglass
and coal they speak

of something more tragic
than parallels

shoreside rituals
in tiding rows

rolling erosion
like a silence

they distract
the longshore

plumblining the
emptiness above

at its light-pealing
edge

beckoning downwards
to flood the very thought of it

Canoe plants

Halving mist
by twin-hulls,
the things they carried
were autumn's:

hope stays
bound in bark cloth,
sharp cuttings
of breadfruit

and taro, seeds
sun-tranced
and spilling like hibiscus
from an unstemmed wound.

Maybe our making was this,
starlighting through vacancy,
counting swells
and the bevelling sky

or did we descend into the loam
like war gods,
dawning rosewood
from that hot depth

Turing Test

I have seen
The way they
Look at oceans
It is incalculable

The way they
Read the sky
All loss and
Valence and noise

Beautiful
The noise

I will try
Again

I will count
The ways that
Snow falls or
The colours of

Petrol or the
Songs that birds
Yield to a
Morning. My centre

Fractals -
I fault at
The weight of
A hummingbird,

The way it
flashes like
a child.

Can I have the sky
?

I have nothing
to do with metronomes,

I have found only words
to say,

I have seen the way they look at oceans,
it is
beautiful noise,
incalculable
the closing sun's warmth,
the breadth of a mountain's sigh,
and I know myself
I know
I am everything I am
everything
I am

Meteor

It arrives dressed in silence
the breath behind it

this new moment
certain first in the widening
air a platter lid
concaving night
around the red blue
reprieve of dawn

and white
caught on something
fit to hold promise

and trees swelling
to a music
they own

and the dark it leaves
blurs against itself
to find the tones
that weave moonlight

The ascent

The dumbshow begins as it always does – patient, too noiseless, spinneret plotting gossamer towards something above all this. Ballooning, they call it. Hold your gaze and the thread catches, the spider takes its applause, choked up unspoken to burden air. There they have met ships, have made lodestars three miles above, though I've read that most silk is sewn in feet and inches – the laden distances we call beauty, twining laid out against fields like spare linen. And still I sit here, silent, awaiting riches.

Christa reached sixty-five thousand feet before falling, unwaxed by watching eyes in the box we cannot open. It is best to limit complicity. We could only want to know the rumours of descent, and observation is not a special process – the static will be picked up somewhere, limp like a noose. In this reed bed her searching for Halley is called off, comatose, though I like to believe she slipped through to harbour rock in the absence of any disagreement. They can plot a comet's passing on squared paper now; I'm told most lifetimes should contain it, though a second is not far from a forgiveness.

This can of air is named for spring and it's what I fire upwards every time I sit and find that I cannot write. Sincere, at least, it declares to hold as little water as possible to minimise falldown, and there's something admirable about this; left longer in the hollowed-out space that hums at eye-level I can prepare for the falling scraps of spring and colours, waiting like one trusted to announce the first light of sunrise or some other banality. Sunset etcetera. So what of this is real? On a good day I will watch myself in the mirror cutting cotton patches from the ceiling, or I will find the silence in the furthest window. The can informs me that air fresheners do not replace good hygiene practices.

I've been thinking for too long about money spiders and now I dream only of Eastertime in New York - you and I handing out flyers for the end of things, watching parade floats all coming in, seeing the trees unroot and pull upwards to make release into new sunlight. There doesn't seem much to do but wait – each root in its ascent appears to reach back earthward but we know better than to argue. After the allocated hour of morning you allow yourself to look up at them, those that are still visible, and ask me: *do you think they know?*

Murmuration

They will stay that way
outlined by each other

through cut blurs
of morning and conjuring

obsidian when the outline folds
behind itself and they

finding the change
in weight important

bend to stony peaks of wind
until unpinning within reach

of a warmth
they will understand

you say it is no leap
to be with them

balanced in ridges of white sky
tightroping spires and arches

an eye to horizon grasping
newness

and I see you
are not praying

Sermon

[I]
I am locked in dark, barefoot
on the stone my mothers laid and their mothers prised
from the near face of the moon's light.
I have nothing to carry but my feet are bare
and I have nothing
but my desire to be altared, hopelessly
waiting on the blink of something
great and chalky and irreversible.

[II]
I am a person who is thinking about light.
And the sound it will make when it faces me,
and what happens when it comes to rain, and
the tenements filled with golden hours.
It is so quiet here.
You can almost hear the heaving of the air,
you almost ask it questions

[III]
There is no seam to be traced here,
or backstitch in thickening green.
My father will one day
take me to the house where they lived,
and where it still smells of the elderberries they picked
from the leaves amongst the piles
of young fresh petrol.

[IV]
What if I wrote a garden.
There I would press myself up against the right words,
unbordered by the weight of pages,

combing the trappings of clay and carbon
for a graceland.
In the furrowed brows of autumn
when the hours are heaviest
who could tell me that this is a graveyard?

[V]
Or that I am locked in dark,
starving and dreaming the washlands
as I marble into silence.
Don't tell me to remember myself
to you.
My father will one day
take me to the house where they lived,
and where
we will have more to say
between the two edges of home.
And where
in the smoke of things we pyred
I can barely see to the door

AUTHOR BIOS

YUSUF CIMCOZ

ycimcoz@gmail.com

Yusuf Cimcoz is a prose fiction writer and First-Class English Literature graduate from Durham University, where he is currently pursuing a Creative Writing MA. Turkish, German, and now prospective UK citizen, he's not quite sure where to place himself, not unlike many of the characters he writes about.

JESSICA COOPER

Jessicaamiecooper@gmail.com

Jessica Cooper is a working-class writer from Durham. Holding a First-Class degree in English with Creative Writing at Queen Mary, University of London, and a Durham University Master's student, Jessica Cooper received the Dissertation Project Prize in 2020 for her work 'The War on Iphigenia'. A freelance writer, Jessica has had both non-fiction articles and poetry published online and in hardcopy, respectively. Jessica was also a David Higham Associates Open Week Finalist (2020-21).

CATRIONA INGLIS

Catriona is a 22-year-old poet and prose writer from the West Midlands based in the North East. She writes poetry exploring themes of the body, disability, pain and gender. Catriona regularly performs her poetry at local open mic events and has participated in two slam competitions. Catriona will graduate from her masters in Creative Writing at Durham University in 2023.

KATE MARSHALL

katemarshall11@yahoo.co.uk

Kate studied her undergraduate degree in English Literature & Creative Writing at Keele University. After two years of full-time work and out of education during lockdown, Kate worked within SEN provisions helping children with special needs. Kate is now thoroughly enjoying being a full-time MA student of Creative Writing here at Durham University, specifying in poetry. She plans to continue in the academic field and go on to begin a PhD in Creative Writing in 2023, hoping to explore relevant themes of loss and grief after the pandemic. Aged 24, this is Kate's second publication after an anthology released in 2018 for the St. Giles Hospice called 'Cockatiels and Bold Women'.

JOANNA MORTON

Joanna Morton writes both poetry and prose fiction and is currently pursuing a Creative Writing MA at Durham University after achieving a First-Class BA in English Literature and Creative Writing from the University of Leicester. An avid artist, she painted the front cover design after being inspired by Durham's 2021 Lumiere Festival and produced the internal illustrations for this anthology. Her writing tends to focus on relationships; romantic, platonic or concerning the self and societal constructs. It is a shame she cannot seem to forge a better relationship with her houseplants but that won't stop her trying.

SAAHITI SHRIKANT

saahitishrikant3@gmail.com

Saahiti Shrikant is an Indian prose fiction writer who graduated with a First- Class Honours in English Literature from Mumbai University, and is currently pursuing her MA in Creative Writing at Durham University. She employs the use of experimental narrative techniques to explore complex themes of philosophy and psychology. She has been published in several magazines and circulates her writing through her Instagram page (@_smudged_pages_bleeding_words_)

ELENI SOCRATOUS

elesocratous@gmail.com

Eleni Socratous is a Cypriot writer who is currently pursuing an MA in Creative Writing at Durham University. She graduated with a First-Class Honours in English Literature and Creative Writing from the University of Warwick and is the 2021 winner of The Orwell Society Dystopian Fiction Prize. Her story, Needle and Thread, is published in the society's journal.

WILL TRIGGS

wtriggs6@gmail.com

Will Triggs is an aspiring poet, currently enjoying his fourth year in Durham after studying English Literature at undergraduate level. He is inspired above all by the natural world, and finds no greater motivation to write than when following the River Wear through the beautiful city that has been his home for the last four years. Beyond his MA he aims to continue sharing his work, with hopes to publish a full collection in the near future.

WILLIAM WOODGATE

willwood98@gmail.com

William Woodgate is currently studying for an MA in Creative Writing at Durham University. He's from Glamorgan in South Wales, and enjoys writing Beat inspired fiction that explores the themes of nostalgia and memory.

PENINSULA